TOP TEN REASONS TO DUMP TRUMP IN 2020

Kelly Hyman

Published by
Hybrid Global Publishing
301 E 57th Street, 4th fl
New York, NY 10022

Copyright © 2019 by Kelly Hyman

All rights reserved. No part of this book may be reproduced or transmitted in any form or by in any means, electronic or mechanical, including photocopying, recording, or by any information storage and retrieval system, without the written permission of the Publisher, except where permitted by law.

Manufactured in the United States of America, or in the United Kingdom when distributed elsewhere.

Hyman, Kelly
    The Top Ten Reasons to Dump Trump in 2020
    LCCN: 2019914957
    ISBN: 978-1-948181-82-2
    eBook: 978-1-948181-83-9

Cover design by: LongBar Creative Solutions (LongBarCreatives.com)
Interior layout and design by: Claudia Volkman

kellyhymanauthor.com

To all Americans, and especially the Millennials, who are passionate about social issues, dedicated to being authentic, and committed to positive change. It's important to make your voice heard. The link to register to vote and check your registration is https://www.usa.gov/register-to-vote. I hope that this book will inspire everyone who reads it to vote, to encourage your friends, family, and colleagues to vote, and to understand that voting matters. Your vote matters.

CONTENTS

Introduction   1
#1: The Lies   7
#2: Human Rights Violations   13
#3: Weakening Endangered Species Protections   21
#4: Environmental Protection Rollbacks   27
#5: Immigration   33
#6: Conflicts of Interest   39
#7: Fake News   45
#8: Cabinet Vacancies   51
#9: Not Fit to Lead   55
#10: The Russia Investigation   61
Conclusion   67
Acknowledgments   69
Notes   71
Resources   87
About the Author   91

INTRODUCTION

IN THE UNITED STATES, we have the right to choose our leaders and participate in issues we care about. Our voices impact the world around us. By getting involved on all levels—family, community, national, international—together we can achieve great things. But we need to vote. Voting matters. We know this, but in the 2016 election, only 60 percent of those who were eligible cast a vote. This was not an all-time low, as social media claimed, but it's nowhere near the numbers we could have.

If there's one thing that's certain, it's that no one can be sure what the outcome of the 2020 election will be. After Donald Trump won the presidency in 2016, the world felt as though it had stepped back in time. In the years that Trump has been president, he's done many things that are unpresidential, to say the least—obstructing a Department of Justice investigation, giving aid and comfort to neo-Nazis and white supremacists, and viciously tearing young children away from their asylum-seeking parents. And most recently, during a call with Ukrainian President Volodymyr Zelensky, he is said

The Top Ten Reasons to Dump Trump in 2020

to have pressured Zelensky to get involved in the United States presidential election by checking into Joseph Biden and his son Hunter over Hunter's past business interests.

"I'm leading in the polls," Trump told reporters when questioned about the call. "They have no idea how they can stop me. The only way they can try is through impeachment." And finally, the House is going forward with an impeachment inquiry.[1]

After this announcement, former ten-day White House communications director, Anthony Scaramucci, said Trump is "gone."[2] In fact, Scaramucci has been doing all he can to ensure his prediction comes true. In an August podcast interview, he said he could sway 5 percent to 8 percent of Trump voters against him—more than enough to win the election.[3]

I don't believe that Scaramucci's prediction about Trump being history will come to pass. Yes, the Intelligence Committee will submit a report of its findings to the House Judiciary Committee, which will draw up the articles of impeachment. But then the next step is the Senate. No Senate has ever voted to remove a president from office (Andrew Jackson and Bill Clinton were not convicted, and Nixon resigned). And this Senate will not convict him. It will be up to us, the American people, to ensure he's not reelected in 2020. And how do we do this? By voting!

In this book, I want to increase your awareness of why

Introduction

Trump is in no position to lead our country. He's shown atrocious judgment—inviting the Taliban to Camp David, engaging in a self-defeating trade war, openly singing the praises of brutal dictators. His racism, bullying, misogyny, and xenophobia is off the charts and totally misrepresents who we are as a country. He's cried "Fake News," at every turn. He's completely incapable of making decisions about the most serious issues that come across his desk. He's totally ignorant of the history and policies of the country he attempts to govern. He can't find rhyme nor reason in the intelligence and information he's given daily. He's impulsive, vindictive, narcissistic, misogynistic, predatory. Remorse and empathy are beyond his grasp. He believes he's "the chosen one," and as such, what's good for Trump is good for the country, if not the universe. With that mindset, anything flies. He's totally unpredictable—and extremely dangerous given his power. It's time for change.

We've shown that in the face of blatant injustice, we can band together, rise up, and affect change. We need to do that now. It's totally within our power to remove Trump. Look at what we've done while he's been in office. Judges defy him. States sue him. His own District of Columbia has sued him. And the Women's March instantly became an annual worldwide event. That 2017 march was the largest single-day protest in history. (How fitting that it happened one day after Trump's sold-out, standing room only, humongous, biggest-*ever*-in-history inauguration attendance.)

Each of the ten chapters in this book outlines a reason not to vote for Trump. While there are far more reasons not to vote for Trump, I've chosen to focus on what I believe to be the top ten. In the Resources section at the end of this book, you'll find organizations you can contact to take part in turning this ship around, including where to register to vote or check to make sure you're registered. Here's what I want you to get out of this book: Whether you're Democrat, Republican, or Independent, Trump is not the right choice. It's time to put our country over the party and do what is best for our country. It's not a party issue (Trump goes after all parties—anyone who criticizes him or doesn't agree with him); it's an *us* issue. Everyone is worse off with Trump—women, men, all ethnicities, farmers, industrialists, steelworkers, coal miners—everyone except Trump. Think about it. Just because Trump says something a few times, it doesn't make it true. We deserve better. Our country deserves better. Anyone who votes for Trump is voting against their own interests. Trump has only one interest—Trump.

Trump is unfit to lead. No matter who you are, your party, or your interests, get out and vote in 2020. Vote, vote, vote. Vote for a candidate who cares about the people of this country and of the world, a candidate who cares about our planet, who treats all humans—no matter their

Introduction

race, religion, sex, or gender identification—with kindness, dignity, and respect. Someone who takes the stewardship of this nation and this planet seriously. We deserve better . . . you deserve better.

#1: THE LIES

WHY WOULD IT BE disastrous if Trump wins in 2020? Let's start with the lies. The constant, brazen, bald-faced lies he lets fly day in and day out, to the point where we can hardly believe a single word of what he says or tweets. As of August 5, 2019, Donald Trump has managed to lie an average of thirteen times per day since he took office.[1] That's 12,019 false statements. Trump lies. About everything from President Barack Obama not being born in the Unites States to supposedly wiretapping his phones in Trump Tower, to losing the popular vote due to voter fraud, to fake praise from the Boy Scouts—the lies keep coming. Objective facts don't seem to matter to Trump at all. He makes up the world as he goes along, citing facts that aren't facts. It doesn't matter as long as they meet his agenda of always being the hero, of always winning, of always being right.

Many have been simply ludicrous and ridiculously transparent. At his energy speech in Monaca, Pennsylvania, he proudly stated: "And we have the cleanest air and water we've ever had in our country right now. The cleanest we've ever had."[2] This is totally false. In 2018, three of the six

The Top Ten Reasons to Dump Trump in 2020

pollutants identified by the Clean Air Act as toxic to human health were in fact higher than they were before Trump took office.[3]

And Sharpie-gate! To cover his blunder of including Alabama in the states threatened by Hurricane Dorian (Alabama was *not* at risk, according to both the National Weather Service and National Hurricane Center), he held up his Sharpie-altered weather map to show how correct he'd been about the storm's path. He also insisted on the weather bureau retracting their statement that Alabama was not at risk. As if that's not frightening enough, the National Oceanic and Atmospheric Administration (NOAA) issued a statement disavowing the comment. Where are our checkpoints if federal agencies can be bullied into swearing that the emperor's wearing new clothes (made in the US)? What—and whom—can we believe?

The lies get more dangerous. One of the things Trump misleads his followers about the most is immigration and our need to keep rapists, gangs, criminals, and rapists outside our borders (when very few of those are attributed to immigrants) and the border wall he promised his voters during his 2016 campaign. The most common falsehood he's told was that the border wall was already being built by the government (first Mexico's, then ours), when only maintenance and minimal additions had been done. Yet now that lie will become a reality. He's taking nearly $4 billion to build 175 miles of his wall by gutting Pentagon

#1: The Lies

funds previously designated for military construction projects, including military base schools, "to boost his own ego," as Senator Chuck Schumer said.[4]

What about the economy being "the best it's ever been"? Wrong. Growth since 2009 is 25 percent, which doesn't come close to the best. In the 1980s, growth was 38 percent, and in the 1990s, it was 43 percent. Sure, unemployment is way down. But that's not because everyone's happily digging coal, drilling oil, and building cars to meet EPA emissions rollbacks. It's because people are dropping out of the workforce, either giving up or become card-carrying members of the gig economy.[5]

Trump has also lied about the Mueller "witch hunt." He claimed the cost to citizens was $40 million during the two years of the inquiry, when the cost was closer to $12 million.[6] He tweeted that "Robert Mueller would have brought charges, if he had ANYTHING, but there were no charges to bring!" Again, not true. Mueller's hands were tied by longstanding Justice Department guidelines stating that a sitting president can't be indicted. (More about the Russia investigation in #10.)

Now, from the Democratic perspective, it's very clear how often Trump makes false claims. The real problem lies within the fact that most of his supporters seem to believe the majority of his lies (and this from a base dominated by evangelical Christians, who are taught that lying is a sin). This has a lot to do with where people get their news and information, and whether those sources are actually credible, something not always considered. People tend to get their news from sources they agree with.[7]

Trump has coined the term "Fake News" to combat reports on his falsehoods, instead accusing credible news sources of telling falsehoods about his falsehoods. This tangled mess of accusations has only made the situation more difficult.

We also have to consider that his base knows he's lying but doesn't care. This in turn can be due to the following reasons:

- the lies confirm their beliefs about issues such as immigration and the need to do something about it;
- the truth of what he says doesn't matter to them nearly as much as the indication that he believes as they do;
- he is achieving the policies they've wanted for so long in social and policy issues; and
- the belief that "we're winning."

Researchers have found that Republicans are more likely than Democrats or Independents to consider outright lying morally acceptable for politicians, a belief primarily driven by Trump right-wing supporters' endorsement of his authoritarianism. In one study, participants were given three scenarios. In all three, a politician lied about an upcoming increase in the unemployment rate. In one scenario, the lie was overt. In another, the lie was by omission. Another

#1: The Lies

used a truthful statement to mislead. Participants then rated each statement from ethical to unethical, dishonest to honest, and immoral to moral. They then indicated their party affiliation. The results were as stated above. When it comes to Trump's base, he can get away with lying and still retain their support.[8]

Democratic discourse is only possibly if everyone agrees on the basic facts of the world around them. Opinions can vary, but not facts. But with each of Trump's lies, the foundation teeters. There has been conjecture about why Trump lies—everything from being a pathological liar, to being just plain deceitful and dishonest, to not even knowing the difference between facts and the world he wants to see. No matter the reason, he's dangerous. He has the power to spread misinformation and convince vulnerable people that it's all true. And he does spread misinformation, largely through Twitter. Never before in our country's history has a president had such direct, unfiltered, and immediate access to the public.

What can we do? As good citizens, we cannot swallow all that's fed us. We must investigate, research, and discuss ideas, leaders, and actions. We need to read, listen, think, speak out. We don't have to get Trump to admit the truth. That won't happen. But we can't stay quiet. We can't let it go. The presidency has been revered and respected throughout history, and we cannot allow a man like Donald Trump to continue defacing the reputation of this great nation.

#2: HUMAN RIGHTS VIOLATIONS

SINCE HE WAS SWORN into office on January 20, 2017, President Donald Trump and his administration have worked tirelessly to implement policies that undermine fundamental human rights—171 as of August 28, 2019.[1] In fact, there have been so many, it's been difficult to choose which ones to highlight here, but some of the more recent violations of the Trump administration include:

- refusing to respond to UN investigators over potential human rights violations in the United States;
- proposing a rule to cut more than 3 million people from the Supplemental Nutrition Assistance Program (SNAP), or food stamps; and
- announcing that some children born to US military members and government employees working overseas wouldn't automatically be considered US citizens.[2]

The United States director of the Humans Rights Watch,

The Top Ten Reasons to Dump Trump in 2020

Nicole Austin-Hillery, said in commenting on the World Report 2019, "For the second year running, the Trump administration assaulted human rights in the US and abroad with an array of policies that harmed refugees, immigrants, women, and many others."[3]

Some of Trump's most controversial human rights rollbacks have stemmed from his harmful immigration policies, including the travel ban targeting mostly Muslim countries, separating children from their parents after crossing the US border and seeking asylum, and the 2017 decision to end the Deferred Action for Childhood Arrivals (DACA) act.

This executive order suspended the issuing of immigrant and nonimmigrant visas for five Muslim-majority countries—Libya, Iran, Somalia, Syria and Yemen—plus North Korea and Venezuela. Bans affect those seeking asylum, including the at-risk Christians in the Middle East Trump swore to protect. It also affects science and the tech industry. In Silicon Valley, 60 percent of workers in STEM jobs with a bachelor's degree or higher were born outside the US in 2017.[4] More than half of the top American tech companies were founded by immigrants or the children of immigrants. Apple, Amazon, Google, and Facebook were all founded by first- or second-generation immigrants.[5] Now, two years after the ban was instated, tech and science are worried about the effect of cutting off talent, as top engineers are opting for other countries.

#2: Human Rights Violations

Zero-Tolerance Policy

In April 2018, then-Attorney General Jeff Sessions signed into effect a zero-tolerance policy. "If you cross this border unlawfully, then we will prosecute you," Sessions said. "If you are smuggling a child, then we will prosecute you, and that child will be separated from you."[6] As a result, thousands of children were torn from their parents or guardians at the US-Mexico border and placed under the supervision of the US Department of Health and Human Services. In June of that year, President Trump rescinded the order due to national and international criticism. US District Judge Dana Sabraw ordered the children to be back with their families within thirty days, but it took longer than that. It turns out there was no plan for reunification. Today, though, all those nearly three thousand children have been reunited with a parent or relatives.[7]

An internal government report found that during the Trump administration, thousands more children may have been separated from their families than the previously reported figure of nearly three thousand. Officials are unsure of the exact number. As of July 2019, seven hundred families fleeing violence and natural disasters for the safety and possibilities of the "shining city on the hill" have been separated since the policy was rescinded.[8]

It gets worse. Reports state that children who were—and still are—kept in detention centers lack access to basic hygiene products such as toothbrushes and soap, and regularly must sleep on cold floors in overcrowded cells.[9] They're often not equipped with blankets, and the temperatures are freezing.[10] They frequently are crawling with lice.[11] Since April 2018, five children have died in detention centers.[12]

The End of DACA

Nine months after he entered office, President Trump terminated the Deferred Action for Childhood Arrivals (DACA) program that President Barack Obama created in 2012 through executive action after Congress refused to pass legislation to grant young immigrants permanent legal status. The program allowed undocumented immigrants, who were brought to the United States when they were young children, often referred to as Dreamers, to be temporarily shielded from deportation and allowed to live and work legally in the country.

Congress once again has the opportunity to permanently protect millions of Dreamers, many of whom have lived in this country for decades. The latest version of the Dream and Promise Act—a bill that's been in litigation for two decades—passed the House in June 2019. This bill would place millions of young undocumented immigrants and immigrants with temporary status on a pathway to US citizenship. Although a recent CBS news poll showed that 87 percent believe that DACA is good for America,[13] it's doubtful it will pass the Republican-ruled Senate, with Mitch McConnell, the self-proclaimed "grim reaper" of Congress, vowing to thwart all progressive proposals on the Senate floor.

#2: Human Rights Violations

There are 3.6 million dreamers in this country, and 800,000 in the DACA program.[14] What happens to them with DACA rescinded, their permits expiring in 2020, and the Dream and Promise Act most likely dead in the water? Do we boot them out of the only country they've ever known and send them "home"? Trump's comments?

> What I'd like to do is a comprehensive immigration plan. But our country and political forces are not ready yet.
>
> There are two sides of a story. It's always tough.

With Trump's love of chaos and keeping others in a state of uncertainty, he seems just fine with leaving Dreamers and their families in limbo.

LGBTQ Rights

Trump hasn't only gone after those who aren't citizens (including their children); he's stripping the rights of more than 50 percent of US citizens—both those who identify with a gender other than their original biological one and women. The Trump administration began targeting LGBTQ rights as soon as he entered office. On his first day, all mentions of LGTBQ issues were removed from the White House website.[15] Since then, the administration has targeted LGTBQ service members, attempting to ban them from serving in the military, even if they are willing to risk their lives for their country.

The Trump administration also proposed a controversial policy that no longer protects gay and transgender workers from discrimination. The memo refers specifically to Title VII of the Civil Rights Act of 1964. In that memo, *sex* is understood to only mean "biologically male or female."[16] And that's not the end of it. The Department of Housing and Urban Development proposed a change to the Equal Access Rule in May 2019 that would allow homeless shelters to deny access to transgender people on religious grounds.

Women's Rights

President Trump has also been launching a steady stream of attacks on women's rights during his time in office, which should be no surprise. He's a misogynist, sexualizes his daughters, has been accused by twenty-five women of sexual misconduct, and bragged to Billy Bush of *Access Hollywood* that he's "a star" with women and, because of his status, can "grab them by the pussy" whenever he wants.

Trump started by attacking Planned Parenthood for their involvement in abortions, even though the clinic provides PAPs, cancer screenings, contraception, and many other women's health services.

His administration has implemented a domestic gag rule that would bar organizations that provide abortion referrals from federal family planning funds, preventing organizations like Planned Parenthood from receiving federal funding under Title X, the program that provides birth

#2: Human Rights Violations

control and other health services to poor women. Planned Parenthood has stated that it will withdraw from the federal program rather than comply with the gag rule on referrals, though it's not clear how they'll make up the funds.

Trump reinstated a "global gag rule" that prohibits foreign NGOs from using US family planning aid to perform or promote abortion, then expanded the law to include global health aid to foreign NGOs, and *then* expanded the law even further, so that organizations that give money to foreign NGOs that perform abortions would not be eligible for US health aid.[17]

In September 2017, the Department of Education announced that it was rescinding Obama-era guidelines on sexual assault in schools, narrowing the definition of sexual harassment and increasing the burden of proof in assault claims.[18]

The human rights violations listed here only graze the surface of all those made by the Trump administration thus far. The only way to ensure that these horrible violations stop and return to the humanitarian policies we've practiced in the past, is to make sure Trump is not reelected in 2020.

#3: WEAKENING ENDANGERED SPECIES PROTECTIONS

THE TRUMP ADMINISTRATION has done serious harm to some important progressive steps taken during the past ten to twenty years in terms of human rights. But their policies have also been harmful in terms of environmental protections, and most recently, moves to weaken endangered species protections.

Specifically, the Trump administration is moving forward on an overhaul to the United States environmental infrastructure. They want to weaken the Endangered Species Act (ESA) and allow more oil and gas drilling, no longer requiring companies to consider the impact this drilling would have on the environment.

The ESA, passed in 1973, is for the conservation of endangered and threatened species and the ecosystems they depend on. The ESA places restrictions on a range of activities involving endangered and threatened animals and plants to help ensure their continued survival. Currently 2,417 plants and animals are protected under this act both in the United states and abroad.[1] This law has saved 99 percent of the endangered species on its list from extinction, including the bald eagle, grizzly bear, and the humpback whale.

Agencies use Environmental Protection Services (EPS) regulations to help determine which habitats to protect so endangered species have the best chance to survive. The overhaul to the ESA would completely change this process, reserving all protections to the "rarest species" rather than as many species as possible. Trump's new regulations would also make it harder to add endangered species to the list and easier to take them off. And more evidence will be required to prove that a species is threatened or endangered.[2]

According to a United Nations report published in May 2019—the Intergovernmental Science-Policy Platform on Biodiversity and Ecosystem Service's (IPBES) Global Assessment Report on Biodiversity and Ecosystem Services—one million of the planet's eight million species are threatened with extinction. The key causes are shrinking habitat, exploitation of natural resources, climate change, and pollution. These factors threaten more than 40 percent of amphibians, 33 percent of all coral reefs, and more than a third of all marine mammals.[3] The changes make it harder to argue that climate change poses a risk to a species' survival. At the same time, the global climate crisis is picking up speed.[4]

Currently, under the law, all threatened species (one step down from endangered) have most of the same protections as endangered species. Soon, though, threatened species

#3: Weakening Endangered Species Protections

will be considered on a case-by-case basis, taking into account how much it might cost to protect a species. In other words, if the cost to business is too great, the species doesn't make the cut. The administration is spinning the ESA changes as an attempt to "modernize" and "improve" implementation of the law.[5] They claim the changes will lift the burden of regulations on business while continuing to protect endangered and threatened species. But think about it. If it's easier to drop species from the list, then their once-protected habitat becomes available for digging up more fossil fuels that contribute to pollution and climate change, which in turn threatens more species, who will be bumped to allow more drilling.

The Endangered Species Act helps protect ecosystems that support those species. In turn, those species can help keep the air and water we depend on clean while also lowering costs on things like asthma and immune-mediated diseases caused by, or triggered by, pollution.[6,7] These ecosystems absorb climate change-causing pollutants like carbon dioxide. Plants absorb the gasses, but animals, including those protected under the Endangered Species Act, play a key role in keeping ecosystems intact. In 2018, another IPBES study showed that nature provides roughly $24 trillion in free ecosystem services in the Americas alone.[8] Is the Trump administration factoring in that $24 million when they determine which animal or plant costs too much to save? Not likely.

The Top Ten Reasons to Dump Trump in 2020

The 2019 IPBES report is a summary for policymakers, a 1,500-page aggregate of the results of thousands of scientific studies on biodiversity loss and how to address it.[9] The results are shattering. Twenty percent of all known species have become extinct in the past century, and the trend is accelerating as the climate changes, which puts more pressure on the fields, fisheries, and the farms that feed the people of our planet.[10] The loss of ecosystem is already impacting 23 percent of the world's farms, and the loss of bees and other pollinators is threatening up to $577 billion in annual crop production. As plants and animals disappear, ecosystems such as rainforests, grasslands, rivers and streams, and coral reefs disappear. And we lose. Because as these ecosystems are destroyed, their services are destroyed, services such as the storage of carbon in plants, soils, geologic formations, the ocean, coastal protection, and water filtration.

Looking at the UN report, it's crystal clear that protections need to be strengthened, not weakened. "For a long time, people just thought of biodiversity as saving nature for its own sake," said IPBES Chair Robert Watson. "But this report makes clear the links between biodiversity and nature and things like food security and clean water in both rich and poor countries."[11]

The final rules are being challenged in court for violating the Endangered Species Act's mandate to prevent extinction and recover listed animal and plant species. While the ESA

#3: Weakening Endangered Species Protections

rollback may not survive in court, the legal process could take years to resolve. In the meantime, the Trump administration can give the all-clear to polluting industries' projects at the expense of endangered species.

The CEO of The Nature Conservancy commented on the UN report: "In the face of these alarming trends, business-as-usual is not an option. Charting a sustainable path will require more funding and collaboration than ever before. The Nature Conservancy scientists have run the numbers: a more sustainable world is still possible if society makes big changes within the next decade—but time is running short. People and nature can both thrive, but only if we take action right now." [12]

Right now. If we fail to act now to protect our planet, it could ultimately have a grave impact on humans and food supply if animals and plants continue to face extinction.

#4: ENVIRONMENTAL PROTECTION ROLLBACKS

IT'S NO SECRET THAT President Donald Trump doesn't believe in climate change; he's made it very clear. Four years before he was elected, President Trump called climate change a "hoax" invented by China (he later retracted that statement). Since taking office, he suggested to the National Republican Congressional Committee that wind turbines are not only annoying but also cause cancer. And people living near the turbines have complained of "tinnitus, raised blood pressure, heart palpitations, tachycardia, stress, anxiety, vertigo, dizziness," but not cancer.[1]

He's wiped any mention of climate change from government websites. The Environmental Data & Governance Initiative (EDGI), which "analyzes federal environmental data, websites, institutions, and policy to improve environmental data stewardship and promote environmental health and environmental justice," found that of the "thousands of websites we monitor, use of the terms 'climate change,' 'clean energy,' and 'adaptation' dropped by 26% between 2016 and 2018, while catch-all terms that are employed to undermine clear analysis—such as 'energy independence,' 'resilience,' and 'sustainability'—increased by 26%. Over half of all pages where 'climate change' was completely removed (73/136) were U.S. Environmental Protection Agency (EPA) pages."[2]

In case erasing words from our country's vocabulary isn't enough of a shell game, Trump has dismissed conclusive findings by top world scientists. He completely dismissed the Intergovernmental Panel on Climate Change (IPCC) special report, which he claimed to have glanced through. When asked what he thought of the report, he said, "It was given to me. It was given to me. And I want to look at who drew it. [Did he not see who'd drawn it up when he supposedly glanced through it?] You know, which group drew it. Because I can give you reports that are fabulous, and I can give you reports that aren't so good." The report drew on data from 6,000 studies conducted by the IPCC—the world's leading scientific body on the subject of global warming. Had he not heard of them? Ninety-one authors and editors from forty countries drafted the report, which was then reviewed by thousands of government and technical experts.[3] It's legit.

When Trump was asked about the findings in the Fourth Annual Climate Assessment,[4] that unchecked global warming would damage health and cost the US hundreds of billions of dollars per year, he said, "I don't believe it." Thirteen federal agencies, including NASA and

#4: Environmental Protection Rollbacks

the Department of Defense, and three hundred scientists wrote this report. And to be clear, it was produced by *our* government. But what do they know? Trump doesn't believe them. Case closed.

His administration has sought to roll back key climate regulations at every turn. As of this writing, Trump has instilled forty-five complete rollbacks, with thirty-five in process, coming to a total of eighty-four rollbacks currently in motion.[5] The rollbacks are predominantly in air pollution, emissions, infrastructure, and planning. They also include drilling and extraction, water pollution, and toxic substance safety. These rollbacks will work quickly to contribute to the climate change we're seeing by increasing greenhouse gas emissions even further.

Here are some more of his frightening rollbacks:

- Rescinding regulations to limit methane emissions despite four gas companies and auto manufacturers going against this.[6]
- Opening public lands and waters offshore to gas and oil drilling. The Trump administration is moving to open millions of land and water offshore to oil and gas drilling.[7]
- Reducing two of Utah's national monuments, Grand-Staircase Escalante (51 percent) and National Monument and Bear Ears (85 percent), opening the nearly two million retrieved

acres to oil and gas development, though both are being challenged in court.[8, 9]
- Pushing to open Alaska's Arctic National Wildlife Refuge and offshore waters in the Arctic and off the East and West coasts to oil and gas exploration.[10]

Altogether, the Trump administration's environmental rollbacks could significantly increase greenhouse gas emissions and lead to thousands of extra deaths from poor air quality every year, according to a recent report prepared by New York University Law School's State Energy and Environmental Impact Center.[11] However, that isn't important to Trump. Instead, he would rather shape environmental protections that better suit him, the fossil fuel industry, and other big businesses he seeks to protect. Time and time again, he's proven he's more concerned about profitability than protecting the planet.

Trump infamously withdrew from the Paris Climate Agreement, (the final withdrawal won't take effect until 2020), the global action plan meant to combat climate change. Their long-term goal is to keep the increase in global average temperature to well below 2 Celsius (35.6 Fahrenheit) above pre-industrial levels; and to limit the increase to 1.5 Celsius (34.7 Fahrenheit), which would reduce the risks and effects of climate change substantially. Nearly two hundred countries came together to form this agreement to take drastic steps to save the planet, collectively.

#4: Environmental Protection Rollbacks

When Trump announced that the United States would no longer be a part of the agreement, it was clear he planned to dismantle years of environmental policy.

At the 2019 G7 Summit, Trump skipped out on a meeting about climate change, claiming he had to meet with the leaders of Germany and India, who must have missed the memo because German Chancellor Angela Merkel and Indian Prime Minister Narendra Modi were in the meeting Trump didn't bother to attend.[12]

President Trump has made it clear to the world that he will always put *his* interests before the interests of the country, and even the planet. He and his administration have worked diligently to undermine years of environmental activism, no matter the cost. Trump is not fit to be president. We need a leader who cares about the people in this country, the world, and the planet we inhabit.

#5: IMMIGRATION

PRESIDENT DONALD TRUMP HAS never been afraid to speak his mind, especially when it comes to one of his major policies—immigration. Since he first announced his candidacy in the 2016 election with a controversial speech declaring that Mexican immigrants are mostly rapists,[1] it was obvious to people who were not his supporters that we had a serious problem on our hands.

Trump recently lit into four progressive representatives—representatives Alexandria Ocasio-Cortez (D-NY), Ayanna Pressley (D-MA), Ilhan Omar (D-MN), and Rashida Tlaib (D-MI). He tweeted that they were from "countries whose governments are a complete and total catastrophe" and that they should "go back" to those countries and "help fix the totally broken and crime-infested places from which they came."[2] Aside from these comments being horribly racist, except for Omar, these congresswomen were born in the US. (But what do facts have to do with it?)

John Roberts, a reporter for Fox News, asked Trump if it bothered him that "many people saw that tweet as racist and that white nationalist groups are finding common cause with you on that point?" Trump replied, "It doesn't concern me, because many people agree with me." In other words, his base agrees with him. A base that has shrunk to 24 percent of those who voted for him or have spoken approvingly of him to pollsters, those who would support him no matter what.[3]

This logic is just plain upsetting, to say the least. Aside from his racist fear-mongering, the United States Equal Employment Opportunity Commission (EEOC) website lists the phrase "Go back to where you came from," as discriminatory in the workplace. Trump is empowering people to hate. It's a primary example of unlawful workplace misconduct. Apparently, these rules don't apply to him because he thinks is above the law, but no one is above the law.

Then he went after Elizabeth Warren's presidential campaign, where she spoke of her Native American ancestry. He tweeted: "Today Elizabeth Warren, sometimes referred to by me as Pocahontas, joined the race for president. Will she run as our first Native American presidential candidate, or has she decided that after 32 years, this is not playing so well anymore? See you on the campaign TRAIL, Liz!"[4] "TRAIL" seems to be a reference to the Trail of Tears—a horrific act of ethnic cleansing in the 1830s century that removed 100,000 Native Americans from their ancestral lands, causing thousands of deaths, so we could take their land for ourselves.

During a meeting of the national security team, Trump read aloud a document listing how many immigrants had

#5: Immigration

received visas to enter the United States in 2017. Fifteen thousand people came from Haiti. "They all have AIDS," he said. Forty thousand came from Nigeria. Two officials reported Trump as saying they would never "go back to their huts" once they saw America.[5]

Speaking in a bipartisan meeting about immigration, attendees said Trump spoke out about Haiti and African countries. "Why are we having all these people from shithole countries come here?" he asked. He then reportedly suggested that we should take more people from countries like Norway. So this seems to be how it plays out: ban people from countries whose population is primarily black; welcome people from countries whose population is primarily white.

This racism is not new. In 1973, in one of the biggest cases of the time, the Department of Justice sued Trump, his father, Fred, and their company for racial discrimination because they wouldn't rent the apartments in Trump Village to African-Americans. In typical Trump fashion, he and his father denied all culpability and attacked their attackers—they sued the United States Government for $100 million. An agreement was reached, but Trump and his father made it clear their agreement was not an admission of guilt.[6] Since taking office, President Trump has demonstrated his racism countless times, and due to his power, these hateful words have been transformed into harmful immigration policies that will plague our country for years to come.

The Top Ten Reasons to Dump Trump in 2020

New rollouts have recently come out that are even more exclusionary than the last. The administration is calling it the "Public Charge" rule. This rule will deny green cards to any migrants who are deemed likely to use welfare, while favoring migrants who have good educations and demonstrate self-sufficiency in their finances. This rule completely removes hope from migrants coming from southern Latin countries whose economies are poor and no longer gives them the opportunity to make a better life for themselves and their families.

The latest evaluating factors for migrants will include credit scores, income level, and potential debt. It will also take into account medical conditions that could become a burden to taxpayers, making it a clear attack on sick and poor people. The road to United States citizenship is long, challenging, and winding, and these regulations will just make it even more difficult for people to legally enter the United States.

Our government is also making it extremely difficult, if not impossible, for those seeking asylum to find refuge here. The Trump administration announced a tightening of restrictions for those seeking asylum, stating they must seek protection in the first country they travel through. This ruling prevents most Central American immigrants, who are fleeing violence and poverty, from seeking asylum in the United States.[7] It also prevents asylum seekers from Africa, Asia, and South America who regularly arrive at the US-Mexico border.

#5: Immigration

Trump's most recent immigration policy and his tightening asylum restrictions could alter the way American immigrants look, literally. Under these policies, it's expected that most European and Canadian immigrants will meet the new requirements more frequently than migrants coming from Mexico and the Caribbean, not to mention Central and South America, Africa, and Asia. This is a clear demonstration of the Trump administration deliberately targeting people with darker skin tones.

Trump is trying to change history and what it means to be an American, completely ignoring the fact that our ancestors all brought us to this country by immigrating. During Trump's time in office, the government agency in charge of granting citizenship to prospective Americans has removed a passage from its mission statement that describes the United States as "a nation of immigrants," and added the mission of "securing the homeland, and honoring our values."[8] Donald Trump challenges everything we stand for and replaces what we as a country have long valued with values that, moral and ethical or not, he and his shrinking we'll-vote-for-you-even-if-you-shoot-someone-on-5th-Avenue base agrees on.

#6: CONFLICTS OF INTEREST

PRESIDENT TRUMP HAS BEEN an extremely controversial president since he took office. His administration has clogged the news headlines every single day with yet another story of his lies, harmful immigration policies, environmental rollbacks, and of course, his conflicts of interest. Unfortunately, he's kept people so busy that sometimes these conflicts seem to fall by the wayside.

Merriam Webster defines *conflicts of interest* as "a conflict between the private interests and the official responsibilities of a person in a position of trust." As of this writing—two years and seven months into Trump's term—an in-depth study conducted by Citizens for Responsibility and Ethics in Washington (CREW) reported more than 2,310 conflicts—all a direct result of President Trump's decision to retain his business interests.[1,2] Trump claims that as president, he's allowed to do so because "the president can't have a conflict of interest."[3] That's not exactly true. According to the 1978 Ethics in Government Act, high-ranking federal officials must disclose their financial holdings and recuse themselves from any government business in which they, their families, or close associates have a financial interest.[4] However, Title 18 Section 208 of the US code declared the president and vice president exempt from conflict-of-interest laws because the presidency has so much power that any possible executive action might pose a potential conflict.[5]

It was expected that these officials would act with the highest integrity, and since President John F. Kennedy's assassination, presidents Lyndon Johnson, Jimmy Carter, Ronald Reagan, George H.W. Bush, Bill Clinton, and George W. Bush have divested their business interests, putting them into an irrevocable blind trust while they were in office. An irrevocable blind trust cannot be modified or dissolved. "The trustor and the beneficiary are usually one in the same, so when the potential conflicts of interest that warrant the blind trust are gone, they can reclaim their assets."[6]

Trump is the exception. Just before his inauguration, he turned over management of the Trump Organization to his two eldest sons and a longtime company executive through a revocable and non-blind trust, meaning he can change the terms, reclaim assets transferred to the trust, or terminate it at any time.[7] While Trump says his sons are running his company, his federal financial disclosure forms show he continues to draw income from the Trump Organization's businesses (including his hotel in Washington). But since Trump refuses to release his returns, complete transparency into his business dealings is impossible.[8]

#6: Conflicts of Interest

According to CREW, who can report only what's documented, Trump's refusal to release his business interests has created the staggering amount of conflicts of interest (outlined below).[9] Some of the biggest include:

- Three-hundred-sixty-two visits were made by President Trump to Trump businesses at taxpayers' expense.
- At least 250 administration officials—including high-level White House staff, members of Trump's cabinet, and individual agency employees—have visited Trump properties 630 times.
- Sixty-three political events, hosted by political groups, have been held at Trump properties.
- Eighty-two events held by special interest group were hosted at Trump properties.
- Fifty-nine foreign trademarks were granted to Trump businesses.
- Ninety members of Congress have made 188 visits to Trump properties, instead of pushing back on President Trump's refusal to divest from his business.
- Nearly six million dollars was spent by political groups at Trump properties. In the ten years before 2016, no more than $100,000 per year was spent.
- One-hundred-fifty-nine of Trump's tweets mentioned one of his properties. Members of

the Trump administration have mentioned a Trump property sixty-five times, sometimes in the course of their official duties.

- Twelve events have been hosted at Trump properties by foreign governments and foreign government-linked organizations.
- One-hundred-eleven officials from sixty-five foreign governments have made 137 visits to Trump properties, each of which is likely a violation of the Emoluments Clause of the United States Constitution. The clause, in Article 1 of the United States Constitution, states: "No Title of Nobility shall be granted by the United States: And no Person holding any Office of Profit or Trust under them, shall, without the Consent of the Congress, accept of any present, Emolument, Office, or Title, of any kind whatever, from any King, Prince, or foreign State." Since this clause was written 230 years ago, it has not been disputed in court, so there are no rulings about what the founders meant. As a result, federal courts have moved extremely slowly as they try to make sense of this unchartered territory.[10] In the meantime, Trump does whatever he wants to.

It seems that time and time again President Trump has based his decisions solely dependent on his own bottom line, without considering the American people he is meant

#6: Conficts of Interest

to be speaking for. With mysterious foreign meetings happening in privately owned Trump properties, no one can truly be sure whether his political policies are in line with his bank account or with the country he swore on oath to protect.

What is for sure is that we need to elect a new leader in 2020. President Trump has proven over the past two years that he believes conflicts of interest and the law don't apply to him. We need a president who we can hold accountable to make this country a better place.

#7: FAKE NEWS

IT HAS BEEN IMPOSSIBLE TO escape the constant cries of "fake news" that have littered our news streams during the past few years. Beginning during his 2016 presidential campaign, Donald Trump began calling all negative press written about him and his business practices "fake news," and has continued to do so during his time in office. Essentially, anything that Trump does not consider to be a glowing review of him is dubbed "fake news." In two interviews—one with Fox business host Lou Dobbs and once with Mike Huckabee with the Trinity Broadcasting Network—Trump claimed that he coined the term, boasting about how proud he was that it had caught on.[1,2]

Trump's claim is, once again, false. He didn't coin the term he's so proud of. According to a Merriam-Webster post, "*fake news* appears to have begun seeing general use at the end of the 19th century," a century after the word *fake* came into use. Before that, the term *false news* was often used.[3] False claims to fake news aside, what does the term really mean? While the term may seem like a harmless, funny quip to use during conversations, the term has actually facilitated a direct attack on the free press and everything it stands for.

Jim Acosta, reporter and author of *The Enemy of the People: A Dangerous Time to Tell the Truth in America,* wrote about how Trump supporters, reacting to his "volatile rhetoric," have caused journalists to feel "endangered." He referred to the "death threats streaming into the social media accounts of news anchors and reporters who cover Trump on a regular basis." He's received his share.

Trump began using the term "fake news" at the same time disinformation campaigns began spreading like wildfire during the 2016 presidential race, further adding to the confusion and legitimately fake news stories that were being actively shared all across Facebook to sway the election in Trump's favor. These attacks have continued relentlessly, escalating as federal investigations began looking into his campaign "strategies" and potential Russian influence, as well as his continuously low approval rating, and have now developed into a real problem.

Trump continuously attacks the free press, including NBC News, ABC News, CBS, CNN, and countless others. He constantly claims that the professional journalists in these newsrooms are writing lies about him, his accomplishments, and his administration. He even went as far to call them "the enemy of the people" in a tweet: "The FAKE NEWS media (failing @nytimes, @NBCNews, @ABC, @

#7: Fake News

CBS, @CNN) is not my enemy, it is the enemy of the American People!" he wrote.[4] This is dangerous talk.

As the 2020 election approaches, Trump is making fake news his primary scapegoat, a call to unite against the media. "Our real opponent," he wrote, "is not the Democrats, or the dwindling number of Republicans that lost their way and got left behind. No, our primary opponent is the Fake News Media." This was attached to a rant about what he calls the "LameStream Media," attacking its alleged lack of sources and fact-checking. "They are now beyond Fake," he wrote; "they are Corrupt."[5] And how does that track with this tweet posted two weeks earlier stating that "journalism . . . is nothing more than an evil propaganda machine for the Democratic party"?[6] It doesn't—first the Democrats are perpetrators of fake news and then innocent victims of the same? But it does track with Trump's pattern of generating chaos, suspicion, and doubt, of attempting to convince the American people of the one true voice in the midst of such turmoil—his. And he lies.

The problem with the president, someone who holds immense influence over the country and its people, calling accurate news stories "fake news" is that he creates a profound distrust that causes his supporters to believe only the outlets that support his views. Not everyone in the country understands journalist practices and integrity. They don't understand the importance of sourcing information from credible news sources, ultimately ending up with a total disarray of information.

I'm not denying that the media needs readers, viewers, and advertisers. I'm not denying that fear sells (Trump certainly uses it to his own advantage), and that sensationalism exists. One of my favorite examples of attention-grabbing headings is from the film *The Shipping News*. Veteran newsman Quoyle (Kevin Spacey) instructs new hire Wavey (Julianne Moore) about writing headlines. He points to the horizon where dark clouds loom and suggests the headline "Imminent Storm Threatens Village." And if there's no storm? "Village Spared from Deadly Storm."[7]

We expect inflated headlines and teasers that promise more than they deliver to keep us tuned in, but at the core of reporting, we also expect that the ethics of the Society of Professional Journalism are adhered to:

Seek the truth and report it. Ethical journalism should be accurate and fair. Journalists should be honest and courageous in gathering, reporting and interpreting information.
Minimize Harm. Ethical journalism treats sources, subjects, colleagues and members of the public as human beings deserving of respect.
Act Independently. The highest and primary obligation of ethical journalism is to serve the public.
Be accountable and transparent. Ethical journalism means taking responsibility for one's work and explaining one's decisions to the public.[8]

#7: Fake News

So has Trump completely destroyed our trust in journalistic integrity? The results are mixed. A 2018 poll conducted by Quinnipiac University showed that when asked "Which comes closer to your point of view: the news media is the enemy of the people, or the news media is an important part of democracy?" 65 percent of U.S. voters said the media is an important part of democracy.[9] Fifty-one percent of Republican's surveyed consider the news media the "enemy of the people," while only 36 percent of Republicans thought the media was "an important part of democracy." Five percent of Democrats believed the media to be the enemy and 91 percent felt they were an important part of democracy.

Another report by the Knight Foundation published that same year showed that while 69 percent of U.S. adults, including more than nine in ten Republicans, say they've lost trust in the news media in recent years, 69 percent of those who have lost trust say that trust can be restored.[10]

It may take some time to reverse the damage, but it can be done. This attack on the press will continue until President Trump leaves office, and the American people elect a leader who is ready to fight with them and work with the press to make this country a better place.

#8: CABINET VACANCIES

THERE HAVE BEEN MANY mishaps in the Trump administration over the past few years he has been in office. While some people are now convinced of his need to be impeached, he still has some public support from his followers keeping his chances of reelection possible. It's now up to the American people to stand up against his administration and start having conversations about where his presidency went wrong and why we must elect a new leader in 2020. One of the most important reasons not to reelect Trump is the vacancies on his cabinets, and the dangerous precedent they set.

Trump entered the summer of 2019 with the most extended cabinet vacancies than any other U.S. president. He has already accumulated more than four times as many days with a vacant Cabinet position than any other president since Ronald Reagan at this point in their presidencies.[1] The longest vacancies within his cabinet include the EPA administrator, UN Ambassador, White House Chief of Staff, Secretary of Defense, Secretary of Homeland Security, Secretary of Veteran Affairs, and the Secretary of Health and Human Services.

The Top Ten Reasons to Dump Trump in 2020

From ethics scandals and ineffective leaders who couldn't manage the large bureaucracies of the federal government to high turnover, Trump's cabinet has been a nightmare. Nine Cabinet officials have left the Trump administration since 2017, either through resignations or by firing, according to data from the Brookings Institution. John F. Kelly was promoted. Former Pentagon Chief Jim Mattis resigned in protest. And Tom Price, Rex Tillerson, David Shulkin, Ryan Zinke, Alex Acosta, Jeff Sessions, and Kirstjen Nielsen resigned under pressure.[2] "Trump's Cabinet turnover at 30 months has exceeded his five predecessors' after an entire first term in office," said Kathryn Dunn Tenpas, who oversees the Brookings data. "It is exceptional."[3]

"There are a lot of qualified people out there, but not a lot who would want to work in this administration given the brevity of tenure that most of these folks face," said Jeremy Bash, who served as chief of staff to former Defense Secretary Leon Panetta. "It's always a gamble when you select people for very senior jobs who have zero experience in government."[4]

But Trump has gotten around the issue of his secretaries being suitable for office by appointing acting officials rather than filling his vacancies with nominations that need Senate approval. The Federal Vacancies Reform Act of 1998, or FVRA, allows presidents to designate "acting" replacements in the event of a Senate-confirmed individual's death, resignation, or incapacitation. They can retain their position for 210 days without having to go through a confirmation

#8: Cabinet Vacancies

hearing, and 300 days if it's the first year of the administration. During that time, if the Senate rejects a nomination for a permanent replacement, the acting secretary can serve an additional 210 days. If a second nomination process fails, the acting secretary can serve a final 210 days more.[5]

Trump is working the system. He's said that he prefers acting Cabinet members. "I like acting. It gives me more flexibility. Do you understand that? I like acting.[6] While an acting Cabinet may give Trump more flexibility, it can also create some instability within the departments, because acting officials often lack the power to resist pressure from the White House, and instead are likely to be more agreeable to do Trump's bidding for him.

There are many reasons why appointing acting officials can be dangerous. First and foremost, acting secretaries don't require Senate confirmation. This allows Trump to name acting officials as he pleases, regardless of their credibility or experience in their newly appointed roles, a practice that's especially beneficial to him in areas such as immigration and trade where there's opposition in the Republican ranks. These malleable department heads have allowed him to enact his most controversial policies, from immigration, to ecology, to health. He also uses filling Cabinet positions with acting secretaries to demonstrate the power of the Executive branch over Congress.

Ultimately, Trump believes cabinet vacancies serve his interests, not the interest of the American people. An acting

The Top Ten Reasons to Dump Trump in 2020

Cabinet is good for Trump, because an acting Cabinet reports only to him. Not appointing secretaries can be harmful to the checks and balances that are systematically built into our government to maintain a sense of fairness. Without those checks and balances, there is the potential for real harm to be done in the way of policy. It's time to elect a new president who respects the office they hold, and the American people.

#9: NOT FIT TO LEAD

PRESIDENT TRUMP'S CURRENT approval rating sits around 40 percent. But if you were to ask him, he would tell you he was the most liked president in history. He's also the most successful president in history, with the best policies in history, with the highest approval rating in, you guessed it, history. No one loves and supports women more, no one is fairer, no one is smarter, no one the least racist—the list goes on and on.

His favorite place to share these tidbits that he's construed completely within his own mind is his Twitter account. Trump uses the platform to directly address, without filter, the nation and the world in a way that has never been done before, with good reason. Because there are no specific policies set in stone as to how to police the president's Twitter account—especially when, because of his office, his tweets are considered "newsworthy"—Jack Dorsey and others at Twitter who call the shots have instead decided to do absolutely nothing except make some of his tweets harder to find.[1] Twitter said it will "place a notice" on such tweets in the future and require users to click through a screen before reading it.[2]

The Top Ten Reasons to Dump Trump in 2020

Twitter has acknowledged that some unnamed "government officials and public figures sometimes say things that could be considered controversial or invite debate and discussion."[3] Perhaps tweets insulting a nuclear-outfitted and seemingly trigger-happy dictator, say, the Supreme Leader of North Korea, would fall into that category: "Why would Kim Jong-un insult me by calling me 'old,' when I would NEVER call him 'short and fat?' Oh well, I try so hard to be his friend—and maybe someday that will happen!"[4]

Because Twitter chooses to do nothing, Trump can do anything he wants. He can attack political leaders, as he did in his tweet to Iranian President Rouhani: NEVER, EVER THREATEN THE UNITED STATES AGAIN OR YOU WILL SUFFER CONSEQUENCES THE LIKES OF WHICH FEW THROUGHOUT HISTORY HAVE EVER SUFFERED BEFORE. WE ARE NO LONGER A COUNTRY THAT WILL STAND FOR YOUR DEMENTED WORDS OF VIOLENCE & DEATH. BE CAUTIOUS!"[5]

Trump can threaten to deploy nuclear bombs: "Just heard Foreign Minister of North Korea speak at U.N. If he echoes thoughts of Little Rocket Man, they won't be around much longer!"[6]

He can make fun of or outright blast United States politicians: "Lightweight Senator @RandPaul should focus on trying to get elected in Kentucky—a great state which is embarrassed by him."[7] And their children: "@

#9: Not Fit to Lead

MeghanMcCain was terrible on @Five yesterday. Angry and obnoxious, she will never make it on T.V. @FoxNews can do so much better!"⁸

He can (and did) retweet far-right anti-Muslim videos titled "Muslim migrant beats up Dutch boy on crutches!" "Muslim Destroys a Statue of Virgin Mary!" and "Islamist mob pushes teenage boy off roof and beats him to death!"⁹ What was he thinking? His tweets have the power to shape international relations, fuel racial and religious tensions, send stock prices up or down, and stir up the American public.

And then there's his favorite use of Twitter, to attack private citizens, goading his army of followers to back him up and act as his attack dogs, sometimes ruining the lives of innocent, private citizens. Eighteen-year-old college student Lauren Batchelder is one example. In 2015, she stood up at a political forum in New Hampshire and told Trump that she didn't think he was "a friend to women." ¹⁰ The next morning, Trump fired back on Twitter, calling Batchelder an "arrogant young woman"¹¹ and accusing her of being a "plant"¹² from Jed Bush's campaign. Then came the threatening phone calls, often sexual, and similar messages that flooded her Facebook and email inboxes.

Chuck Jones, the president of the local chapter of the United Steelworkers union that represents Carrier Corporation employees in Indianapolis, told *The Washington Post* that the president-elect "lied his a-- off" about the

The Top Ten Reasons to Dump Trump in 2020

number of jobs he claimed to have saved.[13] Trump tweeted: "Chuck Jones, who is President of United Steelworkers 1999, has done a terrible job representing workers. No wonder companies flee country!"[14] Half an hour after Trump's tweet, the union leader's phone began to ring, and ring, and ring. Jones told MSNBC host Lawrence O'Donnell that the calls contained "nothing that says they're gonna kill me, but, you know, 'You better keep your eye on your kids. We know what car you drive.' Things along those lines."[15]

In typical Trump fashion, it's fine for him to attack anyone and everyone, but when he feels as though he's the one being attacked, he has simply blocked users, which is a violation of Twitter's policy: "A critical function of our service is providing a place where people can openly and publicly respond to their leaders and hold them accountable."[16] But far more important, blocking users is a violation of the First Amendment. Perhaps Trump hasn't read it, or he's read it and doesn't believe the rules apply to him. The Bill of Rights, which comprises the first ten amendments to the Constitution, is an important document in American politics because it establishes the rights of all American citizens. The very First Amendment is the Freedom of Speech.

The three-judge panel on the United States Court of Appeals for the Second Circuit in New York ruled unanimously that Trump "cannot exclude some from reading his posts because he doesn't like their views." Judge Barrington D. Parker, one of the three judges, wrote: "The First

#9: Not Fit to Lead

Amendment prohibits an official who uses a social media account for government purposes from excluding people from an 'otherwise open online dialogue' because they say things that the official finds objectionable."[17]

No matter how hard Trump may try to convince us of sky-high ratings, of how beloved, admired, and revered he is, his approval rating has remained one of the lowest in history throughout his term due to the general awfulness of his policies and his character. No amount of tweeting can change that. While his inflammatory, frightening, damaging, World War III-be-damned tweets might be perfectly in line with Twitter's terms of service, it's not appropriate for the "Leader of the Free World."

In his new book, *When at Times the Mob Is Swayed: A Citizen's Guide to Defending Our Republic,* Author Burt Neuborne, one of America's top civil liberties lawyers, questions "whether the federal government can contain Trump and the GOP power grabs." According to his first wife's divorce settlement, Trump even studied and annotated Hitler's speeches. Steve Rosenfeld, the author of the article, cites twenty ways Trump is like Hitler, including both finding "direct communication channels to their base," "demonizing anyone who crosses them, "unceasingly attack objective truth," "attacking mainstream media," and "attacking the judiciary and rule of law."[18]

Trump doesn't follow or believe in the Rule of Law. He debases it with his cheating, lying, ignoring legal requests,

The Top Ten Reasons to Dump Trump in 2020

and publicly denigrating judges. Since the day he's taken office, he's been breaking the law with impunity.

#10: THE RUSSIA INVESTIGATION

BECAUSE THE RUSSIAN INVESTIGATION conducted by Robert Mueller's office was so heavily covered during the past few years, I hesitated to include it in this book. However, the entire investigation—and more important, its findings—are entirely too crucial not to mention, especially because absolutely nothing has been done to ensure this won't happen again in the 2020 election.

Four months after President Trump took office, special counsel Robert Mueller was appointed to oversee the investigation of Russian interference into the 2016 United States presidential election.[1] That probe was completed after twenty-two months of investigating, and a redacted version of the report was released in April 2019.[2] Thirty-four people and three Russian companies were indicted along the way, with seven convicted so far, including former Trump attorney Michael Cohen and former Trump campaign chair Paul Manafort.[3]

There was a lot of confusion when the report was first presented by Attorney General William Barr, who declared in his summary letter that the report cleared Trump of any collusion because Mueller didn't indict him. But this is where it gets messy. The special counsel found that Russia *did* interfere with the election, but he "did not find that the Trump campaign, or anyone associated with it, conspired or coordinated with the Russian government in these efforts, despite multiple efforts from Russian-affiliated individuals to assist the Trump campaign."[4] As far as obstruction, Barr's letter said, "the Special Counsel states that 'while this report does not conclude that the President committed a crime, it also does not exonerate him.'"[5]

Mueller was unable to charge Trump because a prosecutor cannot indict a sitting president. His decision not to indict Trump came despite evidence in Mueller's own final report that the president of the United States was potentially guilty of a crime. However, because he couldn't charge the president, Mueller presented his findings to Congress to allow them to decide whether they wanted to begin impeachment proceedings.

He did say that "generally" Trump wasn't always truthful in answering questions about whether he "sought to use his official power outside of usual channels."[6] Mueller has also stated multiple times since, including in his July 24 testimony before House Judiciary Committee, that if Trump were not a sitting president, he could be charged with obstruction of justice. However, this also gets fuzzy, because there's confusion whether the answer referred to "*a* president" or "*the* president."[7]

#10: The Russia Investigation

Of course, Trump was unhappy that the FBI launched a counterintelligence investigation into Russian interference in the 2016 election and began attacking Mueller immediately. Because Barr presented the report to the press by declaring Mueller's evidence "not sufficient to establish that the President committed an obstruction-of-justice-offence," people still remain confused to this day about what the report actually contains.[8]

Mueller repeatedly affirmed evidence he'd gathered that Trump took actions to impede his investigation, and he refuted Trump's claim that the report showed "no obstruction" and "no collusion." Mueller said he didn't even explore collusion because it's not a legal term.[9] "The president was not exculpated for the acts that he allegedly committed," Mueller told the House Judiciary Committee. "We did not address 'collusion,' which is not a legal term. Rather, we focused on whether the evidence was sufficient to charge any member of the campaign with taking part in a criminal conspiracy. It was not."[10]

Mueller also indulged many of Democrats' characterizations of Trump campaign officials' conduct during the 2016 election. At one point, Mueller even panned the president's own statements, including his encouragement of WikiLeaks' disclosures of hacked Democratic emails. "Problematic is an understatement in terms of what it displays, giving some hope or some boost to what is and should be illegal activity," Mueller said of Trump's repeated praise for WikiLeaks both on Twitter and at his rallies.[11]

The Top Ten Reasons to Dump Trump in 2020

So what does this mean for 2020? Just one day—one *day*—after Mueller spoke with the House Judiciary Committee, Trump was at it again, only this time he was asking Ukraine President Volodymyr Zelensky to investigate his political rivals, in this case, Joe Biden and his son Hunter Biden. Nearly every poll has Biden defeating Trump nationwide and in battleground states. Previously, he'd told Pompeo and Vice President Pence to withhold nearly $400 million in military aid to the Ukraine seemingly to hold out the aid as a carrot for his request, though he claims that's simply to encourage other countries to pitch in as well.[12] This time Trump faces impeachment. If he is impeached and brought to trial, will the Republican Senate convict? Or will Trump walk away free and clear yet again? To convict, the Republican-controlled Senate needs a two-thirds vote. Plus they're not about to push through anything presented by what Fox host Sean Hannity referred to as the "dirtbag" Democrats who are suffering from "mass psychosis." Hannity states unequivocally, "Trump won't be removed from office.[13] They will not convict. No one will go against the party. As Cindy McCain said in an interview with CNN, "If you're not walking the line, then you're out. That's just not right. That's not the party that my husband and I belonged to."[14] The only way to get him out of office is to vote. And once again, Trump is dealing with impending charges against him by deflecting and going on the attack. This time, he's after Hillary again. The

#10: The Russia Investigation

Trump administration has intensified the email investigation of Hillary Clinton's former aids. So far, they've contacted some 130 officials who sent emails to then Secretary of State Hillary Clinton's private email. The emails have been labeled as classified, after the fact, and represent possible security violations.[15]

He also deflected and attacked the Democratic "savages" on Twitter. "Can you imagine if these Do Nothing Democrat Savages, people like Nadler, Schiff, AOC Plus 3, and many more, had a Republican Party who would have done to Obama what the Do Nothings are doing to me. Oh well, maybe next time!"[16]

Our country is already great. We don't need to make it great *again*. What we need is a great leader. We need a president who's going to unite our country, not divide it. Several polls show that the majority of American's agree with Democrats on the majority of major issues, such as health care, gun control, and the environment.[17] Let us not be divided. Let us unite to do what's best for our country and not reelect Trump. We deserve better.

CONCLUSION

DONALD TRUMP DOESN'T CARE about the people who elected him or the people he's meant to serve in public office. He doesn't care about human rights violations, invoking racist immigration policies, his growing list of conflicts of interests, or saving the planet. The only thing Donald Trump cares about is Donald Trump, which he has proven time and time again. He lies, including about who he is. He paints himself as a self-made billionaire. He's not self-made; he's not the embodiment of the self-made-pull-yourself-up-by-your-bootstraps American. He was earning $200 thousand per year from his dad's business by the time he was three years old and was a millionaire by the time he was eight. From his father's real estate business, he received 413 million in today's dollars. Much of that was through tax dodges in the 1990s.[1] He was never fit to be president to begin with, and he certainly is not fit for a second time. It's time for the American people to elect someone who is ready to do whatever it takes to save the planet we live on and serve the American people.

There's talk that he could lose by five million popular

The Top Ten Reasons to Dump Trump in 2020

votes and still win. And even if he doesn't win, there is speculation about what to do if he won't leave office. He jokes about keeping his seat in the oval office for ten to fourteen more years. So what can you do? First of all, vote. Urge your friends to vote. Volunteer. Drive people to the polls. Learn the issues. Educate others. Approximately 58 percent of people voted in the 2016 election.[2] That's the lowest turnout in twenty years. Let's turn that trend around in 2020. Check the Resources section for more information about what you can do to be a part of the social change we so desperately need. One person can make a difference. Be that person.

ACKNOWLEDGMENTS

WRITING A BOOK IS a team effort, and I'm so grateful for the team I had. This book started out as a series of blogs. Thank you, Amanda, for all your research and help with the blogs. Big thanks to Kelly Malone for your keen editing skills and help in making my words shine. Cyndi Long of LongBar Creative Solutions, you did an amazing job designing the cover of this book. Claudia Volkman, thanks so much for your copyediting skills and for designing and typesetting the interior. Thanks so much to my amazing PR person, Jay Jones, for all your hard work. Darcie Rowan, your belief in this project and your tireless enthusiasm for getting this book out to the public has been such a gift. Karen Strauss, I so appreciate your publishing expertise. And Lil Barcaski, also of LongBar Creative Solutions, thanks for the great job on my author's website. To everyone else who gave their time and energy to this project, thank you. And to all those who took the time to read this book, I hope it's inspired you to take action, to get out and vote! And finally, I would like to specially thank my husband, who inspires me every day.

NOTES

Introduction
1. John Wagner, Scott Clement. "Trump Claims without Evidence That He Is 'Leading in the Polls' as He Pushes Back against Impeachment." *The Washington Post*. WP Company, September 24, 2019. https://www.washingtonpost.com/politics/trump-claims-without-evidence-that-he-is-leading-in-the-polls-as-he-pushes-back-against-impeachment/2019/09/24/71519294-ded8-11e9-8dc8-498eabc129a0_story.html.
2. Mazza, Ed. "Anthony Scaramucci Makes A Bold Prediction About How It Ends For Trump." *HuffPost*, September 25, 2019. https://www.huffpost.com/entry/anthony-scaramucci-donald-trump-done_n_5d89bd9ee4b0c2a85cb04e35.
3. Mazza, Ed. "Scaramucci Reveals Plan To Take Down 'Night King' Trump With 'The Small Hands'." *HuffPost*, August 21, 2019. https://www.huffpost.com/entry/anthony-scaramucci-trump-super-pac_n_5d5cb323e4b0f667ed6a40b1.

#1: The Lies
1. Rozsa, Matthew. "Donald Trump Has Lied an Average of 13 Times a Day since Becoming President, Analysis Finds." *Salon*, August 12, 2019. https://www.salon.com/2019/08/12/donald-trump-has-lied-an-average-of-13-times-a-day-since-becoming-president-analysis-finds/.2.
2. Dale, Daniel, and Tara Subramaniam. "Donald Trump Made 84 False Claims Last Week." CNN. Cable News Network, August 21, 2019. https://www.cnn.com/2019/08/21/politics/fact-check-trump-84-false-claims-last-week/index.html?no-st=1567974077.
3. EPA. Environmental Protection Agency. Accessed September 28,

The Top Ten Reasons to Dump Trump in 2020

2019. https://gispub.epa.gov/air/trendsreport/2018/#summary.

4. Ward, Alex. "The US Military Will Pay for Trump's Border Wall, Not Mexico." *Vox*, September 4, 2019. https://www.vox.com/2019/9/4/20848968/trump-border-wall-mexico-military.

5. Hedrick-Wong, Yuwa. "Trump Says U.S. Economy Is 'Best It Has Ever Been,' But Facts Tell A Different Story." *Forbes. Forbes Magazine*, July 19, 2019. https://www.forbes.com/sites/yuwahedrickwong/2019/07/19/cheap-credit-and-lack-of-competition-gums-up-the-u-s-economy/#1528984e50c7.

6. Cohen, Marshall. "Fact-Checking Trump's Flurry of Falsehoods and Lies after Mueller Declined to Exonerate Him." CNN. Cable News Network, May 31, 2019. https://www.cnn.com/2019/05/30/politics/fact-checking-trump-mueller-claims/index.html.

7. "People Choose News That Fits Their Views." *LiveScience*. Purch. Accessed September 28, 2019. https://www.livescience.com/3640-people-choose-news-fits-views.html.

8. Jacobs, Tom. "Why So Many Trump Supporters Are OK With the President's Lies." *Pacific Standard*, March 14, 2019. https://psmag.com/news/why-so-many-trump-supporters-are-ok-with-the-presidents-lies.

#2: Human Rights Violations
1. "Trump Administration Civil and Human Rights Rollbacks." The Leadership Conference on Civil and Human Rights. Accessed September 28, 2019. https://civilrights.org/trump-rollbacks/#2019.

2. "Trump Administration Civil and Human Rights Rollbacks."

3. "US: Backtracking on Human Rights." Human Rights Watch, May 22, 2019. https://www.hrw.org/news/2019/01/17/us-backtracking-human-rights.

4. Silicon Valley Competitiveness and Innovation Project - 2019 Update. SVCIP, February 2019. https://www.svcip.com/.

5. Saracsalinas. "Mary Meeker Just Presented 294 Slides on the Future of the Internet - Read Them Here." CNBC, May 30, 2018. https://www.cnbc.com/2018/05/30/mary-meekers-internet-trends-2018.

6. "Attorney General Sessions Delivers Remarks Discussing the

Notes

Immigration Enforcement Actions of the Trump Administration." The United States Department of Justice, May 7, 2018. https://www.justice.gov/opa/speech/attorney-general-sessions-delivers-remarks-discussing-immigration-enforcement-actions.

7. Aguilera, Jasmine. "Everything To Know About The Status of Family Separation." *Time*. Accessed September 28, 2019. https://time.com/5678313/trump-administration-family-separation-lawsuits/.

8. Pearle, Lauren. "Trump Administration Admits Thousands More Migrant Families May Have Been Separated than Estimated." ABC News. ABC News Network, February 4, 2019.https://abcnews.go.com/US/trump-administration-unsure-thousands-migrant-families-separated-originally/story?id=60797633.

9. Long, Clara, and Nicole Austin-Hillery. "We Went to a Border Detention Center for Children. What We Saw Was Awful." CNN. Cable News Network, June 25, 2019. https://www.cnn.com/2019/06/24/opinions/children-migrant-centers-at-border-long-austin-hillery/index.html.

10. Valle, Gaby Del. "Flu, Lice, and Open Toilets: What Attorneys Saw at Migrant Child Processing Centers." *Vice*, June 22, 2019. https://www.vice.com/en_us/article/43jpjp/flu-lice-and-open-toilets-what-attorneys-saw-at-migrant-child-processing-centers.

11. Valle. "Flu, Lice, and Open Toilets: What Attorneys Saw at Migrant Child Processing Centers."

12. Goodkind, Nicole. "8-Year-Old Migrant Children Are Being Forced to Care for Toddlers in Detention Camps; Kids Are Being Fed Un-Defrosted Meals, and Infants Don't Have Diapers." *Newsweek*, June 24, 2019. https://www.newsweek.com/migrant-children-detention-camps-donald-trump-1445313.

13. "Most Americans Support DACA, but Oppose Border Wall-CBS News Poll." CBS News. CBS Interactive. Accessed September 28, 2019. https://www.cbsnews.com/news/most-americans-support-daca-but-oppose-border-wall-cbs-news-poll/.

14. Gomez, Alan. "There Are 3.6M 'DREAMers'-a Number Far Greater than Commonly Known." *USA Today*. Gannett Satellite Information Network, January 18, 2018. https://

www.usatoday.com/story/news/nation/2018/01/18/there-3-5-m-dreamers-and-most-may-face-nightmare/1042134001/.
15. "LGBT Rights Page Disappears from White House Web Site." *The Washington Post*. WP Company. Accessed September 28, 2019. https://www.washingtonpost.com/local/2017/live-updates/politics/live-coverage-of-trumps-inauguration/lgbt-rights-page-disappears-from-white-house-web-site/.
16. Bach, Natasha. "When Asked About Human Rights Issues, Trump Pointed to His Website." *Fortune*, July 1, 2019. https://fortune.com/2019/06/21/trump-human-rights-issues-amnesty/.
17. Dharssi, Alia. "Trump's Global Gag Rule Is Killing Women, Report Says." *Foreign Policy*, June 19, 2019. https://foreignpolicy.com/2019/06/19/how-trumps-global-gag-rule-is-killing-women-colombia/?utm_source=PostUp&utm_medium=email&utm_campaign=13745&utm_term=Morning Brief OC.
18. Hefling, Kimberly, Caitlin Emma, and Nancy Cook. "Obama-Era School Sexual Assault Policy Rescinded." POLITICO, September 22, 2017. https://www.politico.com/story/2017/09/22/obama-era-school-sexual-assault-policy-rescinded-243016.

#3 Weakening Endangered Species Protections
1. Kann, Drew. "The Trump Administration Wants to Roll Back the Endangered Species Act. These 10 Animals Might Not Be Here Today without It." CNN. Cable News Network, July 25, 2018. https://www.cnn.com/2018/07/25/politics/endangered-species-act-animals-saved-from-extinction-trnd/index.html.
2. Wallace, Gregory, and Ellie Kaufman. "Trump Admin Moves to Weaken Endangered Species Protections." CNN. Cable News Network, August 12, 2019. https://www.cnn.com/2019/08/12/politics/endangered-species-act/index.html?no-st=1565875533.
3. "UN Report: Nature's Dangerous Decline 'Unprecedented'; Species Extinction Rates 'Accelerating' - United Nations Sustainable Development." United Nations. United Nations. Accessed September

Notes

28, 2019. https://www.un.org/sustainabledevelopment/blog/2019/05/nature-decline-unprecedented-report/.

4. "Who Benefits From an Endangered Species Act Rollback? Big Polluters." Sierra Club, August 13, 2019. https://www.sierraclub.org/sierra/who-benefits-endangered-species-act-rollback-big-polluters.

5. Wildlife Service. "ESA Implementation: Regulation Revisions." Official Web page of the U S Fish and Wildlife Service. Accessed September 28, 2019. https://www.fws.gov/endangered/improving_ESA/regulation-revisions.html.

6. "Ozone Shuts Down Early Immune Response In Lungs And Body." *ScienceDaily*, October 3, 2007. https://www.sciencedaily.com/releases/2007/09/070930083243.htm.

7. Guarnieri, Michael, and John R Balmes. "Outdoor Air Pollution and Asthma." *Lancet* (London, England). U.S. National Library of Medicine, May 3, 2014. https://www.ncbi.nlm.nih.gov/pmc/articles/PMC4465283/.

8. "Assessment Report on Biodiversity and Ecosystem Services for the Americas." IPBES. Accessed September 28, 2019. https://www.ipbes.net/assessment-reports/americas.

9. Foraise, Declan, and Declan Foraise. "Extinction Crisis Threatens Global Food Supplies." *Ecosystem Marketplace*. Accessed September 28, 2019. https://www.ecosystemmarketplace.com/articles/extinction-crisis-threatens-ecosystem-services-provide-food/.

10. "US: Backtracking on Human Rights." *Human Rights Watch*, May 22, 2019. https://www.hrw.org/news/2019/01/17/us-backtracking-human-rights.

11. "UN Report: Nature's Dangerous Decline 'Unprecedented'; Species Extinction Rates 'Accelerating' - United Nations Sustainable Development." United Nations. Accessed September 28, 2019. https://www.un.org/sustainabledevelopment/blog/2019/05/nature-decline-unprecedented-report/.

12. "UN Report Says More Species Threatened With Extinction Than Any Other Time in Human History." The Nature Conservancy.

The Top Ten Reasons to Dump Trump in 2020

Accessed September 28, 2019. https://www.nature.org/en-us/newsroom/un-report-ipbes-biodiversity/.

#4: Environmental Protection Rollbacks
1. Trump, Donald. "Trump's Ridiculous Linkbetween Cancer, Wind Turbines." @politifact, April 8, 2019. https://www.politifact.com/truth-o-meter/statements/2019/apr/08/donald-trump/republicans-dismiss-trumps-windmill-and-cancer-cla/.
2. Malivel, Garance. "The New Digital Landscape: How the Trump Administration Has Undermined Federal Web Infrastructures for Climate Information." EDGI, September 20, 2019. https://envirodatagov.org/publication/the-new-digital-landscape-how-the-trump-administration-has-undermined-federal-web-infrastructures-for-climate-information/.
3. Liptak, Kevin. "Trump Expresses Suspicion about UN Climate Report." CNN. Cable News Network, October 9, 2018. https://www.cnn.com/2018/10/09/politics/donald-trump-climate-report-un/index.
4. Usgcrp. "Fourth National Climate Assessment: Summary Findings." NCA4, January 1, 1970. https://nca2018.globalchange.gov/.
5. Popovich, Nadja, Livia Albeck-ripka, and Kendra Pierre-louis. "85 Environmental Rules Being Rolled Back Under Trump." *The New York Times*, June 2, 2019. https://www.nytimes.com/interactive/2019/climate/trump-environment-rollbacks.html.
6. Popovich, Albeck-ripka, and Kendra. "85 Environmental Rules Being Rolled Back Under Trump."
7. Kann, Drew. "Trump's Rollback of Climate Change Regulations Will Be Felt Far beyond His Presidency." CNN. Cable News Network, September 4, 2019. https://www.cnn.com/2019/09/04/politics/trump-climate-change-policy-rollbacks/index.html.
8. "Trump Shrank This National Monument to Spur a Mining Boom—but Will Those Lost Protections Yield Real Profits?" *The Washington Post*. WP Company, January 15, 2019. https://www.washingtonpost.com/graphics/2019/national/environment/will-anyone-mine-after-grand-staircase-escalante-reduction-by-trump/.

Notes

9. Popovich, Nadja. "Bears Ears National Monument Is Shrinking. Here's What Is Being Cut." *The New York Times*, December 8, 2017. https://www.nytimes.com/interactive/2017/12/08/climate/bears-ears-monument-trump.html.
10. Popovich, Albeck-ripka, and Kendra. "85 Environmental Rules Being Rolled Back Under Trump."
11. Banerjee, Neela, Sabrina Shankman, James Bruggers, Bob Berwyn, Marianne Lavelle, Kristoffer Tigue, Georgina Gustin, Phil McKenna, Kristoffer Tigue, and John H. Cushman Jr. "How Much Would Trump's Climate Rule Rollbacks Worsen Health and Emissions?" *InsideClimate News*, March 7, 2019. https://insideclimatenews.org/news/06032019/trump-climate-regulations-rollback-cost-health-emissions-clean-power-plan-cars-oil-gas-methane.
12. Rozsa, Matthew. "President Trump Skips G7 Meeting on Climate Change, and His Excuse Makes No Sense." *Salon*. Salon.com, August 26, 2019. https://www.salon.com/2019/08/26/president-trump-skips-g7-meeting-on-climate-change-and-his-excuse-makes-no-sense/.

#5: Immigration

1. "Here's Donald Trump's Presidential Announcement Speech." *Time*, June 16, 2015. https://time.com/3923128/donald-trump-announcement-speech/.
2. Trump, Donald J.(@realDonaldTrump). Twitter, July 14, 2019, 5:27 a.m. https://twitter.com/realdonaldtrump/status/1150381394234941448?lang=en.
3. Dean, John, John Dean, and John W. Dean. "Trump's Base: Broadly Speaking, Who Are They?" Verdict Comments, February 16, 2018. https://verdict.justia.com/2018/02/16/trumps-base-broadly-speaking.
4. Trump, Donald J. (@realDonaldTrump). Twitter, February 9, 2019, 2:54 p.m. https://twitter.com/realDonaldTrump/status/1094368870415110145.
5. Michael. "Stoking Fears, Trump Defied Bureaucracy to Advance Immigration Agenda." *The New York Times*, December 23, 2017. https://www.nytimes.com/2017/12/23/us/politics/trump-immigration.html.

The Top Ten Reasons to Dump Trump in 2020

6. Dunlap, David W. "1973: Meet Donald Trump." *The New York Times*. July 30, 2013. https://www.nytimes.com/times-insider/2015/07/30/1973-meet-donald-trump/?_r=0&module=inline.
7. Guardian, agencies and staff. "Supreme Court Decision to Let Trump Deny Asylum Reverses Years of US Policy." *The Guardian*. Guardian News and Media, September 11, 2019. https://www.theguardian.com/us-news/2019/sep/11/trump-supreme-court-deny-asylum-immigrants.
8. Lartey, Jamiles. "Citizenship Agency Removes Description of US as 'Nation of Immigrants'." *The Guardian*. Guardian News and Media, February 22, 2018. https://www.theguardian.com/us-news/2018/feb/22/us-immigration-uscis-mission-statement.

#6: Conflicts of Interest
1. "Report: Trump's Conflicts in Year Two." CREW. Accessed September 29, 2019. https://www.citizensforethics.org/presidential-profiteering-trumps-conflicts-got-worse/.
2. Henderson, Alex, and AlterNet. "Donald Trump Has Had at Least 2,310 Conflicts of Interest during His Presidency, Study Finds." *Salon*. Salon.com, August 23, 2019. https://www.salon.com/2019/08/23/donald-trump-has-had-at-least-2310-conflicts-of-interest-during-his-presidency-study-finds_partner/.
3. The New York Times. "Donald Trump's New York Times Interview: Full Transcript." *The New York Times*, November 23, 2016. https://www.nytimes.com/2016/11/23/us/politics/trump-new-york-times-interview-transcript.html?hp&action=click&pgtype=Homepage&clickSource=story-heading&module=b-lede-package-region°ion&WT.nav=top-news&_r=0.
4. Ribicoff, and Abraham A. "S.555 - 95th Congress (1977-1978): Ethics in Government Act." Congress.gov, October 26, 1978. https://www.congress.gov/bill/95th-congress/senate-bill/555.
5. "18 U.S. Code § 208 - Acts Affecting a Personal Financial Interest." Legal Information Institute. Legal Information Institute. Accessed September 29, 2019. https://www.law.cornell.edu/uscode/text/18/208.
6. "What Is a Blind Trust? Here's Everything You Need To Know."

Notes

Arizona Estate Planning, July 18, 2019. https://www.jacksonwhitelaw.com/arizona-estate-planning/what-is-a-blind-trust/.
7. "What Is a Blind Trust? Here's Everything You Need To Know."
8. Hanssen, Shelby, and Ken Dilanian. "Reps of 22 Foreign Governments Have Spent Money at Trump Properties." NBCNews.com. NBCUniversal News Group, June 12, 2019. https://www.nbcnews.com/politics/donald-trump/reps-22-foreign-governments-have-spent-money-trump-properties-n1015806.
9. "Trump's 2,000 Conflicts of Interest (and Counting)." CREW. Accessed September 29, 2019. https://www.citizensforethics.org/2000-trump-conflicts-of-interest-counting/.
10. Hanssen, Shelby, and Ken Dilanian. "Reps of 22 Foreign Governments Have Spent Money at Trump Properties." NBCNews.com. NBCUniversal News Group, June 12, 2019. https://www.nbcnews.com/politics/donald-trump/reps-22-foreign-governments-have-spent-money-trump-properties-n1015806.

#7: Fake News

1. Ferguson, David. "'I'm so Proud': Donald Trump Tells Lou Dobbs He Invented 'Fake News'." Raw Story, October 25, 2017. https://www.rawstory.com/2017/10/im-so-proud-donald-trump-tells-lou-dobbs-he-invented-fake-news/.
2. Cillizza, Chris. "Donald Trump Just Claimed He Invented 'Fake News'." CNN. Cable News Network, October 26, 2017. https://www.cnn.com/2017/10/08/politics/trump-huckabee-fake/index.html.
3. "How Is 'Fake News' Defined, and When Will It Be Added to the Dictionary?" *Merriam-Webster*. Accessed September 29, 2019. https://www.merriam-webster.com/words-at-play/the-real-story-of-fake-news.
4. Trump, Donald J. (@realDonaldTrump). Twitter, August 18, 2019, 5:22 a.m. https://twitter.com/realDonaldTrump/status/1163063728218263552?s=20.
5. Trump, Donald J. (@realDonaldTrump). Twitter, September 2, 2019, 5:22 a.m. https://twitter.com/realdonaldtrump/status/1168499357131427840.

The Top Ten Reasons to Dump Trump in 2020

6. Trump, Donald J. (@realDonaldTrump). Twitter, August 18, 2019, 5:22 a.m. https://twitter.com/realDonaldTrump/status/1163063728218263552?s=20.
7. Holden, Stephen. "An Outsider Finds His Future by Facing His Past." *The New York Times*, December 25, 2001. https://www.nytimes.com/2001/12/25/movies/film-review-an-outsider-finds-his-future-by-facing-his-past.html.
8. "SPJ Code of Ethics—Society of Professional Journalists." Society of Professional Journalists—Improving and Protecting Journalism Since 1909. Accessed September 29, 2019. https://www.spj.org/ethicscode.asp.
9. Quinnipiac University. "QU Poll Release Detail." QU Poll. Accessed September 29, 2019. https://poll.qu.edu/national/release-detail?ReleaseID=2561.
10. Knight Foundation. "Indicators of News Media Trust." Knight Foundation. Accessed September 29, 2019. https://www.knightfoundation.org/reports/indicators-of-news-media-trust.

#8: Cabinet Vacancies
1. Witherspoon, Andrew. "Trump's Empty Cabinet Positions Have Exceeded Any Recent President, and It's Not Even Close." *Axios*, June 6, 2019. https://www.axios.com/trump-cabinet-vacancies-65a66f00-a140-4b49-887f-3c1bcf6469a7.html.
2. Tenpas, Kathryn Dunn. "Tracking Turnover in the Trump Administration." *Brookings*, September 18, 2019. https://www.brookings.edu/research/tracking-turnover-in-the-trump-administration/.
3. Tenpas, Kathryn Dunn. "Tracking Turnover in the Trump Administration."
4. Johnson, Eliana, Marianne Levine, Eliana Johnson, Wesley Morgan, Connor O'Brien, and David Brown. "Trump's Empty Cabinet." POLITICO, June 18, 2019. https://www.politico.com/story/2019/06/18/donald-trump-empty-cabinet-1369865.
5. "The Federal Vacancies Reform Act of 1998." GSA, August 13, 2017. https://www.gsa.gov/governmentwide-initiatives/presidential-transition/legislative-overview/the-federal-vacancies-reform-act-of-1998.

Notes

6. Becker, Amanda. "Trump Says Acting Cabinet Members Give Him 'More Flexibility'." *Reuters*. Thomson Reuters, January 6, 2019. https://www.reuters.com/article/us-usa-trump-cabinet/trump-says-acting-cabinet-members-give-him-more-flexibility-idUSKCN1P00IG.

#9: Not Fit to Lead

1. Schleifer, Theodore. "Twitter Won't Censor Trump's Rule-Breaking Tweets, but It Will Make Them Harder to Find." *Vox*, June 27, 2019. https://www.vox.com/recode/2019/6/27/18761360/donald-trump-twitter-policy-censorship-rules.
2. Lutz, Eric. "Jack Dorsey Lays the Groundwork to Finally Censor Trump." *Vanity Fair*, June 28, 2019. https://www.vanityfair.com/news/2019/06/jack-dorsey-twitter-may-finally-censor-trump-warning-label.
3. Lutz, Eric. "Jack Dorsey Lays the Groundwork to Finally Censor Trump." *Vanity Fair*, June 28, 2019.https://www.vanityfair.com/news/2019/06/jack-dorsey-twitter-may-finally-censor-trump-warning-label.
4. Trump, Donald J. (@realDonaldTrump). Twitter, November 12, 2017, 4:48 p.m. https://twitter.com/realdonaldtrump/status/929511061954297857.
5. Trump, Donald J. (@realDonaldTrump).Twitter, July 23, 2018, 8:24 p.m. https://twitter.com/realdonaldtrump/status/1021234525626609666?lang=en.
6. Trump, Donald J. (@realDonaldTrump). Twitter, September 24, 2017, 8:09 p.m. https://twitter.com/realdonaldtrump/status/911789314169823232?lang=en.
7. Trump, Donald J. (@realDonaldTrump).Twitter, September 12, 2015, 12:55 p.m. https://twitter.com/realDonaldTrump/status/642788749030608896?ref_src=twsrc^tfw|twcamp^tweetembed|twterm^642788749030608896&ref_url=https://military.id.me/news/the-dirtiest-donald-trump-tweets-according-to-aristocratic-biz-mag/.
8. Trump, Donald J. (@realDonaldTrump). Twitter, September 5, 2015; https://twitter.com/realDonaldTrump/status/640131477179645952?ref_src=twsrc^tfw|twcamp^tweetembed|twterm^640131477179645952&ref_url=https://military.id.me/news/the-dirtiest-donald-trump-tweets-according-to-aristocratic-biz-mag/.
9. Baker, Peter, and Eileen Sullivan. "Trump Shares Inflammatory

The Top Ten Reasons to Dump Trump in 2020

Anti-Muslim Videos, and Britain's Leader Condemns Them." *The New York Times*, November 29, 2017. https://www.nytimes.com/2017/11/29/us/politics/trump-anti-muslim-videos-jayda-fransen.html?src=trending&module=inline&version=context°ion&action=click&contentCollection=Trending&pgtype=article.

10. Johnson, Jenna. "This Is What Happens When Donald Trump Attacks a Private Citizen on Twitter." *The Washington Post*. WP Company, December 8, 2016. https://www.washingtonpost.com/politics/this-is-what-happens-when-donald-trump-attacks-a-private-citizen-on-twitter/2016/12/08/a1380ece-bd62-11e6-91ee-1adddfe36cbe_story.html.

11. Trump, Donald J. (@realDonaldTrump). Twitter, October 13, 2015, 4:39, p.m. https://twitter.com/realDonaldTrump/status/653897939933364224?ref_src=twsrc^tfw.

12. Trump, Donald J. (@realDonaldTrump). Twitter, October 13, 2015, 8:52 a.m. https://twitter.com/realDonaldTrump/status/653961401363468288?ref_src=twsrc^tfw.

13. Seipel, Brooke. "Carrier Union Leader: Trump 'Lied His Ass off' about Deal." TheHill, December 6, 2016. https://thehill.com/blogs/blog-briefing-room/news/309077-carrier-union-leader-trump-lied-his-a-off-about-deal.

14. Trump, Donald J. (@realDonaldTrump). Twitter, December 8, 2016, 4:41 p.m. https://twitter.com/realdonaldtrump/status/806660011904614408?lang=en.

15. "The Last Word with Lawrence O'Donnell, Transcript 12/7/2016." MSNBC. NBCUniversal News Group, December 7, 2016. http://www.msnbc.com/transcripts/the-last-word/2016-12-07.

16. Twitter Safety (@Twittersafety). "Defining Public Interest on Twitter." Twitter, September 29, 2019. https://blog.twitter.com/en_us/topics/company/2019/publicinterest.html.

17. Savage, Charlie. "Trump Can't Block Critics From His Twitter Account, Appeals Court Rules." *The New York Times*, July 9, 2019. https://www.nytimes.com/2019/07/09/us/politics/trump-twitter-first-amendment.html.

18. Rosenfeld, Steven. "Leading Civil Rights Lawyer Shows 20

Notes

Ways Trump Is Copying Hitler's Early Rhetoric and Policies." *Common Dreams*, August 9, 2019. https://www.commondreams.org/views/2019/08/09/leading-civil-rights-lawyer-shows-20-ways-trump-copying-hitlers-early-rhetoric-and?utm_campaign=shareaholic&utm_medium=referral&utm_source=facebook&fbclid=IwAR0k3TO_6ppKUtp2imwradkrbUlasnB7migTYTW-1u7pKSzhkYl53QrDAwI.

#10: The Russia Investigation
1. "2016 Pres. Election Investigation Fast Facts." CNN. Cable News Network, September 16, 2019. https://www.cnn.com/2017/10/12/us/2016-presidential-election-investigation-fast-facts/index.html.
2. "Read the Full, Redacted Mueller Report." *The Washington Post*. WP Company, April 18, 2019. https://www.washingtonpost.com/graphics/2019/politics/read-the-mueller-report/.
3. Jansen, Bart, Tom Vanden Brook, Kevin Johnson, and William Cummings. "Mueller's Investigation Is Done. Here Are the 34 People He Indicted along the Way." *USA Today*. Gannett Satellite Information Network, March 25, 2019. https://www.usatoday.com/story/news/politics/2019/03/25/muellers-russia-report-special-counsel-indictments-charges/3266050002/.
4. "Read the Full, Redacted Mueller Report." *The Washington Post*. WP Company, April 18, 2019. https://www.washingtonpost.com/graphics/2019/politics/read-the-mueller-report/.
5. "Document: Attorney General Barr Letter on Mueller Report." *Lawfare*, March 25, 2019. https://www.lawfareblog.com/document-attorney-general-barr-letter-mueller-report.
6. "Full Transcript: Mueller Testimony before House Judiciary, Intelligence Committees." NBCNews.com. NBCUniversal News Group, July 29, 2019. https://www.nbcnews.com/politics/congress/full-transcript-robert-mueller-house-committee-testimony-n1033216.
7. "Full Transcript: Mueller Testimony before House Judiciary, Intelligence Committees." NBCNews.com. NBCUniversal News Group, July 29, 2019. https://www.nbcnews.com/politics/congress/full-transcript-robert-mueller-house-committee-testimony-n1033216.

The Top Ten Reasons to Dump Trump in 2020

8. "Document: Attorney General Barr Letter on Mueller Report." Lawfare, March 25, 2019. https://www.lawfareblog.com/document-attorney-general-barr-letter-mueller-report.
9. "Full Transcript: Mueller Testimony before House Judiciary, Intelligence Committees." NBCNews.com. NBCUniversal News Group, July 29, 2019. https://www.nbcnews.com/politics/congress/full-transcript-robert-mueller-house-committee-testimony-n1033216.
10. "Full Transcript: Mueller Testimony before House Judiciary, Intelligence Committees." NBCNews.com. NBCUniversal News Group, July 29, 2019. https://www.nbcnews.com/politics/congress/full-transcript-robert-mueller-house-committee-testimony-n1033216.
11. "Full Transcript: Mueller Testimony before House Judiciary, Intelligence Committees." NBCNews.com. NBCUniversal News Group, July 29, 2019. https://www.nbcnews.com/politics/congress/full-transcript-robert-mueller-house-committee-testimony-n1033216.
12. Demirjian, Karoun, Josh Dawsey, Ellen Nakashima, and Carol D. Leonnig. "Trump Ordered Hold on Military Aid Days before Calling Ukrainian President, Officials Say." *The Washington Post*. WP Company, September 23, 2019. https://www.washingtonpost.com/national-security/trump-ordered-hold-on-military-aid-days-before-calling-ukrainian-president-officials-say/2019/09/23/df93a6ca-de38-11e9-8dc8-498eabc129a0_story.html.
13. Garcia, Victor. "Hannity Calls Dems 'Dirtbags,' Says Trump Won't Be Removed from Office." Fox News. FOX News Network, September 28, 2019. https://www.foxnews.com/media/hannity-calls-dems-dirtbags-says-president-trump-wont-be-removed-from-office.
14. Ehrlich, Jamie. "Cindy McCain Says GOP No Longer the 'Party That My Husband and I Belonged to'." CNN. Cable News Network, September 25, 2019. https://www.cnn.com/2019/09/25/politics/cindy-mccain-republican-party-john-mccain/index.html.
15. Miller, Greg, Greg Jaffe, and Karoun Demirjian. "State Dept. Intensifies Email Probe of Hillary Clinton's Former Aides." *The Washington Post*. WP Company, September 28, 2019. https://www.washingtonpost.com/national-security/

Notes

state-dept-intensifies-email-probe-of-hillary-clintons-former-aides/2019/09/28/9f15497e-e1f2-11e9-8dc8-498eabc129a0_story.

16. Trump, Donald J. (@realDonaldTrump). Twitter, September 28, 2019, 5:16 a.m. https://twitter.com/realDonaldTrump/status/1177919923885969408?ref_src=twsrc^tfw|twcamp^tweetembed&ref_url=https://d-14443344752541034256.ampproject.net/1909181902540/frame.html.16.

17. Washington, Focus. "Polls Show Most Americans Agree with Democrats on Major Issues." Focus Washington - Navigating the Swamp, April 9, 2019. https://focuswashington.com/2019/04/08/polls-show-most-americans-agree-with-democrats-on-major-issues/.

Conclusion

1. Barstow, David, Susanne Craig, and Russ Buettner. "Trump Engaged in Suspect Tax Schemes as He Reaped Riches From His Father." *The New York Times*, October 2, 2018. https://www.nytimes.com/interactive/2018/10/02/us/politics/donald-trump-tax-schemes-fred-trump.html.

2. "2016g." United States Elections Project. Accessed September 29, 2019. http://www.electproject.org/2016g.

RESOURCES

VOTE
USAgov. Learn if you're eligible to vote, how to register, check, or change your information. Find the deadline to register to vote in your state: https://www.usa.gov/register-to-vote.

Project Vote Smart. Find voting records, politician biographies and contact information, interest group ratings, a collection of public statements, and campaign finance records. If you're feeling overwhelmed by the sheer number of candidates or are on the fence, the website provides a tool called Vote Easy to help match you to the candidate with the most compatible views: https://www.nypl.org/blog/2016/01/29/tools-informed-voting.

ENGAGE
Common Cause. They're fighting to expand voting rights, eliminate gerrymandering, and pushing for popular vote presidential elections. If you want to volunteer at a Common Cause state office, phonebank, or textbank, organize your

community, write a letter to the editor—they'll help with whatever you need: https://www.commoncause.org/.

Election Protection. The national, nonpartisan Election Protection coalition works year-round to ensure that all voters have an equal opportunity to vote and have that vote count. Get help registering and help others, get an absentee ballot, learn about polling stations and voting rules in your state, report an incident or get assistance. Donate or volunteer: https://866ourvote.org/.

Project Vote. Their key mission is to increase voter participation among historically disenfranchised communities. Low-income citizens, people of color, and Americans under the age of thirty all remain dramatically underrepresented in the American electorate. Find out how you can help: http://www.projectvote.org/issues/civic-engagement/.

Rock the Vote. This nonpartisan nonprofit dedicated to building the political power of young people has registered and turned out millions of young voters on campuses, in communities, and online. They've successfully fought for—and defended—voting rights and increased access to democracy. They've raised awareness and campaigned for issues that impact the lives of young people. And they've pioneered innovative ways to make registration and voting work for our generation, and built open-source technology to empower other organizations too. Join/help out: https://www.rockthevote.org/about-us/.

Spread the Vote. The largest population of voters in America is people who are registered to vote, but don't turnout at the polls. Why not? Challenges with transportation, childcare, voter education, and more keep people from showing up on election day. Spread the vote helps people get voter IDs in states that require them, make election guides that are easy to understand, create digital education tools, and create and execute a plan to vote. Donate or volunteer: https://www.spreadthevote.org/.

Woke Vote. This grassroots organization was a big part of the record black turnout in the midterm Senate elections in Alabama, a state known for its penchant for suppression of voters of color. Woke Vote trains organizers, mobilizes disengaged voters of color, and engages disenfranchised voters of color through strategic social media outreach, campus and faith-based outreach, social impact demonstrations, and intense mobilization (GOTV) efforts. Help out: https://wokevote.us/.

ABOUT THE AUTHOR

ACTING HAS ALWAYS been a passion for Kelly Hyman, who began her career at just five years old. She has enjoyed a lengthy career, bringing the joy of the arts to audiences for nearly twenty-five years. As a young adult, Kelly had the honor of being nominated for a Youth in Film Award. Some of her favorite roles and most memorable work include the part of Loretta on *Young and the Restless* and *Three's Company* star Norman Fell's daughter on the show *Gettin' There*. She worked with the iconic Adam West (known best for playing Batman in the original TV show) while playing the role of Donna in the movie *Doin' Time on Planet Earth*. You might also recognize Kelly's voice from the "Give Me a Break" Kit-Kat ads.

Although her love of the stage will always be something she cherishes, after twenty-five years of devoting her life to her craft, Kelly decided to go to law school, and currently she's working as an attorney. Both these passions in Kelly's life have brought a unique blend of skills, which she's been using to gain traction as a Democratic political strategist and legal analyst and commentator. She's appeared on shows such as *Fox & Friends First*, Fox News' *The Ingraham Angle*, *Law & Crime*, and ABC's *America This Week* with Eric Bolling. Now as a successful businesswoman in two separate industries, Kelly is excited to be joining her talents to leave her mark on the world.

One of the things that drew Kelly Hyman to becoming a lawyer was the ability to bring change in someone's life. (As an attorney, she's been referred to by the media as "the modern-day Erin Brockovich.") The arts have this ability, too, which is a core part of why Kelly has been able to bridge her training so seamlessly. Being able to take these two points of passion to create a new career has been a great joy in Kelly's life. In addition to her acting, she's enjoyed work as a TV personality, lecturer, and speaker. Having the ability to imagine all possibilities, show confidence in business, command the right body language, and think quickly on her toes are skills Kelly accredits to her training as an actress, skills she incorporates into the classes she teaches and the seminars she gives on improv for women in the legal profession. What once seemed like two opposite paths have quickly turned into a wonderfully unique venture for Kelly to explore.

Kelly earned her BA in Communications from the University of California, Los Angeles, and her Juris Doctor degree cum laude from the University of Florida's Levin College of Law. She's involved in a number of political and law-oriented groups and causes to help serve her community—locally and nationally—more fully.

Happily married to the love of her life, Kelly and her husband enjoy traveling the world together whenever they have the chance.

www.ingramcontent.com/pod-product-compliance
Lightning Source LLC
Chambersburg PA
CBHW070032040426
42333CB00040B/1581